T0130501

Memories of
Papa Albert

SHARON BENJAMIN
JAY FOSTER - ILLUSTRATOR

Copyright © 2019 by Sharon Benjamin. 800825

All rights reserved. No part of this book may be reproduced or transmitted in
any form or by any means, electronic or mechanical, including photocopying,
recording, or by any information storage and retrieval system, without
permission in writing from the copyright owner.

This is a work of fiction. Names, characters, places and incidents either
are the product of the author's imagination or are used fictitiously, and
any resemblance to any actual persons, living or dead, events, or locales is
entirely coincidental.

Illustrated by Jay Foster

ISBN: Softcover   978-1-7960-4988-6
       EBook   978-1-7960-4987-9

Print information available on the last page

Rev. date: 08/01/2019

Memories of
Papa Albert

I squeezed my eyes.

I couldn't cry.

My father was crying.

His eyes were red.

Why couldn't I cry?

Wasn't I going to miss Papa Albert?

Didn't I love him, too?

The preacher, family members, and friends talked about how much they loved Papa Albert. They talked about how they would miss him.

I thought about the good memories that I enjoyed with my dear Papa Albert.

Papa Albert was neatly dressed when he went into town.

He seemed taller than anyone else. He walked and said, "Hello," to people on the street.

Lots of people knew "Mr. Marshall." He would say, "This is Sharon, my granddaughter."

That made me smile and
feel very special.

It was so much fun to run around with the chickens as Papa Albert fed them corn kernels.

It was just as much fun watching Papa Albert feed the pigs.

I would sit on the fence and watch them race to the trough to eat.

Papa Albert would get his fields ready to plant seeds. He didn't have a tractor like other farmers.

His mules pulled a plow to till the soil.

After a few
weeks, Papa
Albert had
delicious
watermelons
in his fields.

He would hitch his mules to the wagon
and haul the watermelons to the house.

It was so much fun to ride on
the back of the wagon.

Bumpety, bump!

Bumpety, bump!

The best part was sitting on the front porch with Papa Albert and enjoying the watermelons.

DELICIOUS!

After we filled our bellies with watermelon, Papa Albert and I would sit on the porch and relax. We watched and waited for one special car.

It was the mailman.

He would wave to us.

I would run out to get the mail while
Papa Albert kept on relaxing.

Suddenly, the organist was playing Papa Albert's favorite hymn, "Amazing Grace."

The preacher said, "Amen."

The funeral ended.

Warm tears were trickling down my face - warm tears of joy like the fond

"Memories of Papa Albert"

that I will always have in my heart.

Printed in the United States
By Bookmasters